Whatever Love Means

CHRISTINE NO

BARRELHOUSE BOOKS

Copyright © 2021 Christine No
All rights reserved.

"Katy" from THE COLLECTED POEMS OF FRANK O'HARA by Frank O'Hara, copyright © 1971 by Maureen Granville-Smith, Administratrix of the Estate of Frank O'Hara, copyright renewed 1999 by Maureen O'Hara Granville-Smith and Donald Allen. Used by permission of Alfred A. Knopf, an imprint of the Knopf Doubleday Publishing Group, a division of Penguin Random House LLC. All rights reserved.

Published by Barrelhouse Books
Baltimore, Maryland
www.barrelhousemag.com

No part of this book may be reproduced in any manner whatsoever without express permission, with the exception of brief quotations embodied in critical articles or reviews. For information about reprints, or any other queries, please contact Barrelhouse Books at barrelhousebooks@gmail.com or online at http://barrelhousemag.com.

Published in the United States of America
ISBN 13: 978-0-9889945-9-1

First Edition
Cover art and book design by Shanna Compton

For Grandma & Brandeh

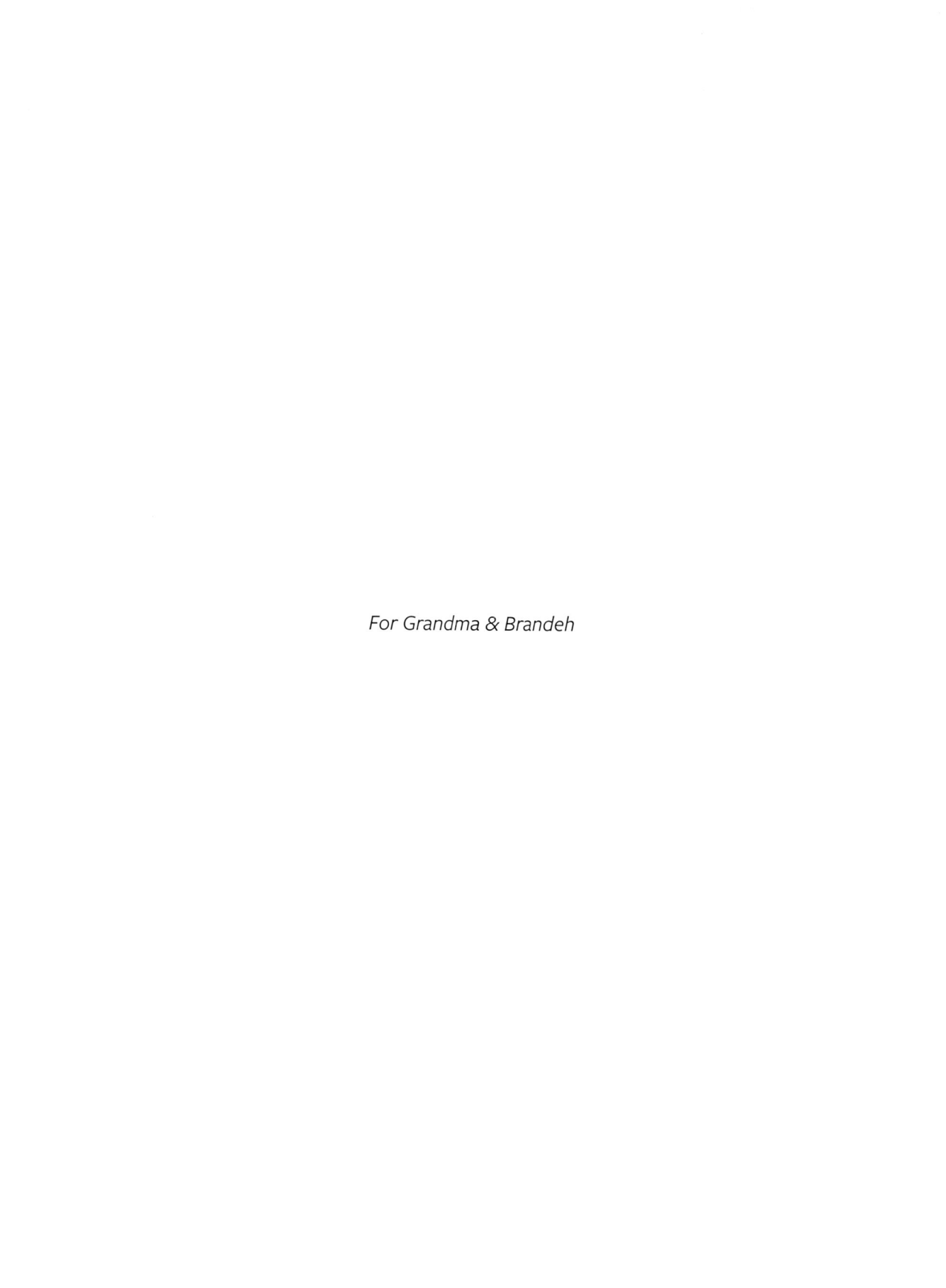

CONTENTS

[I]

9 Dear Joan, Another Birthday
12 Motherhood
13 Visible Body
14 Reminder
15 Bribe
17 Elegy
19 Lesser Gods
20 Snakeskin
22 Groundling
25 Snake Poem / Cento
28 Half Life
30 Red Name
33 A Pigeon Is a Rock Dove

[II]

39 Save Me San Francisco
41 Notes from Hubble's Dream I:
43 Ideation
45 Stars with Teeth
46 California
48 What Happens When Depression Is No Longer Your Singular Universe.

[III]

53 Last Season On
54 Pet Sounds [*Dear Valentine*]
55 To Do List
59 Effigy
62 Patron Saint of the Lost Cause
64 Firework
65 This Is a Poem about Climate Change

- 67   Terminology
- 69   Most Birds Do Not Mate for Life. Not Even a Genuine Pair Bond.
- 72   Iron Maiden
- 73   Bloom
- 76   End of Lease

[IV]

- 79   Lucid Dream
- 80   Albatross
- 82   Psychopomp
- 83   October
- 84   I Refuse
- 85   Salad Days
- 89   At the Motel Behind the Denny's
- 91   You Might Be Dead or Dreaming
- 94   Notes from Hubble's Dream II
- 96   Quantum Entanglement

[V]

- 101   My Grandmother Dreams
- 102   Osip Mandelstam's Egg
- 104   Aubergine
- 106   Amiss
- 108   Prayer for the Season
- 110   Dog Poem

[VI]

- 115   Admission
- 119   Namesake
- 122   Frank

- 125   Acknowledgments
- 127   About the Author

[I]

"We tell ourselves stories in order to live... We look for the sermon in the suicide, for the social or moral lesson in the murder of five. We interpret what we see, select the most workable of the multiple choices. We live entirely, especially if we are writers, by the imposition of a narrative line upon disparate images, by the "ideas" with which we have learned to freeze the shifting phantasmagoria which is our actual experience."

—Joan Didion, "Slouching Towards Bethlehem"

DEAR JOAN, ANOTHER BIRTHDAY

9AM:

They say I should develop my body of work.
I'd look better if I went to the gym,
if I'd written a book in my twenties.

But I am thirty-three today.

I've heard the lecture: that the body fails us,
that failure shapes us.

Can't you see the round of these shoulders,
the disappointment of spine?

Is this not the shape of failure?

My left wrist aches, my right hand a fist.
This pen, this poem, this room, this ruin—

are these not shapes? Shall I further
bend, further story my undoing?

Do you feel it yet?

Have I hurt your feelings?

1PM:

Are you as human as I am
shapeless? Most days,

I manage on Adderall
and coffee—a waste.

Pro tip: the drugs won't take
the neurons won't fire,

Can't run ragged
on empty, already.

12AM:

Another year swallowed.
January cold, almost forty
everything different now.

Remember when
it was cigarettes for breakfast,
spit on the sidewalk, blow and burn
and no bedtime?

I've been an open mouth,
a revolving door, teeth-readied
with the pigeons and strays, all of us
awaiting the second coming,

The Great Redesignation.

I'd like something other than
this hamster run.

I'd like to believe in
God, I don't know what.

Something other than
Other People—

The awful things
they promise, everything
they've taken.

Everything they mean
and refuse to take back.

MOTHERHOOD

Could not bear
the gravitas, the once
impossible—

I've become
an uncomfortable question:

Where would I hide
a body?

This world
an open field

And I, already
an easy target.

VISIBLE BODY

Against a window, the skin gives.
Light and blood, bone and guts,
the scone you had for breakfast,
it's dappled, inconsistent image

We are blood drawn, breath awaiting
another beam illuminating
our molecules dancing away.

Our brief, see-through shapes:
the body mirage, concrete miracle

That we may exist again
as heat, particle and wave, as smoke
and breath. How clouds pass,
their shadows brief. We are shade
and burst.

We are tree. We are red and blue
superhighway—so swift, no spill.
Closer: we are daisy chain
root vine under rib cage,
up bloom two bright lungs.

Closer: your heart, a film frame
a lighthouse, a lantern, a sunbeam
an atlas, a window, the wonder—

REMINDER

My thighs touch too close for comfort.
Hipbones buried in my sides   old handlebars
or the bronze gates   to a woman forgotten.   Pull,
she says   come closer.   I do not bleed   anymore
I maneuver this daunting vessel and   I am starved.
Please   come closer.
I want to disappear with the reptiles.
My large parts dissolved   and leave my bones,
just bones to piece   an entirely new entirety.
Being beautiful is a human   thing.
Being human is not as humane   as one is led to believe.
Last year I was the hurricane   the year before
an asteroid.   This year I am a mammal
who burrows to hide.   I tried to sing   Launched nothing.
No ship or fin or flock. Sometimes   they speak
but not to me.   *I am lonely   please.*
I tried again. Screamed bloody murder.   Woke up still
a woman hell-bent   on her own fantastic demise.
Twice now I've tried   to sever myself gracefully,   perfect
the French Exit   the soft shoe   away
I've screamed.   I've sung.   I've starved myself spotless.
But the fat fingered reminder   I could not manage
even extinction.   I am the remainder   yes I remember:
Stranded vessel   Ill fitting   Stranger
Flesh coat.   *Just wait—*

I'll try it again.

BRIBE

Body rejects copper recoils
metal neat unyielding

Body consumes coil purge
still only meat pieces

Another could have been
someone else

Left the house unhinged
broke the screen door

Dear Body, I am terrified
blood running thick turning

Me inside out doubled
over nails tracing grout

Vomit in the wishing well
more blood rust

Dear Body I have bled alongside
you cried into palms fell asleep
inside my own

Dear Body, I have hands to catch
two *good* hands to carry all bodies
of water made to promise

Should out come silverfish out swim minnows
I will kiss each one I will toss them back

Should out come pennies
they will count

Should they want to leave
I will wish them well I will not
keep them long

ELEGY

I bent form to fit your needs: woodwind, a player piano
a sleeveless dress, your favorite suite?
Stay, Bored Composer.

A venue, then: basilica of knees, a bathroom floor
what cool tiles lie here.

Beneath you I am a deep bow, a shin's kiss.
A prayer: pitch forward, my sorrow prostrate
my reverent forehead, leveled.

That I were a desolate howl, that I were
a ventricle, a blue whale cathedral: echo click,
marble reverb *on and on—*

Long, lonely arc: *Love*
Thud: days and days since—
Anxious: pluck each second,
pedal the organ.

I, practiced form: requiem, memoir, elegy
I, parched wound, I, decomposition.
I, obedient. I, curved.

I got lost.
You buried the lead sheet.

I played too high, too fast and shrill. Showoff
kissed the ceiling, fell wet shameless. Ceaseless
crescendo no apex, I screamed for you:

Brittle songbird fell in love.
Brittle songbird hit the ceiling.

Bored Composer went too far.
Brittle songbird broke in two.

LESSER GODS

Grandma says come the end of days we'll place magnets in our palms, opposite prayer.
The mark of the devil over our third eye, as currency.
That God will destroy the world, again: burn us this time, not drown.

Mom roams the desert: Vegas, Reno—looking for doves / a way back to grace.
Stepfather uses words like *breasts* and *tulip-flowers*.
Grandma says they worship demons & lesser gods.

After dark I look for stars, comets,
my mother's headlights
hurdling here / away.

Pray to God, whichever one,
to torch the Earth.

Take all of us.

SNAKESKIN *am I weak or have we always felt with our whole bodies?*

My grandmother remembers less & little else always wants
Her photo taken needs portraits for her funeral.

This game every weekend, years now
& counting. A little bit of lipstick,
she smiles.

When I could afford it
I brought home jeweled bottles
French names for eternal beauty.

A new year already. My mind blinks
on and off. I write:

When we had money
my mother shed yellow
Chanel, each day worn once—

Leave it be. I write:

My shoulder hurts. I wonder how
I have become so reactive. I worry.

Woman after my mother am I another
woman? What little else beneath these sheaths of slather and zip?
Electric collarbone, a brittle neck adorned—

Go away. I write.

It is cruel to call clutter a sin. Some of us
were raised to disappear. We eke out space
anyway. A lover once called me a series of piles.

In nightmares, I'm naked
in my mother's closet. She, another iteration
stiletto heels and snakeskin, rears up
out of her other selves.

Sloppy Girl—red lips, all spine. Unhinged
her jaw beckons me home.

GROUNDLING

1.

I hold anger like my mother
wedged between shoulder and spine
where wings should have sprouted
but didn't.

Where the nubs grew over, skin and feather
left her back hunched,
her lips pursed,
her gaze flitting elsewhere, elsewhere
but sky.

I hold it like disrupted prayer,
two palms clenched

Or an unfinished poem,
impatient, pacing.

I hold anger like my mother
who did not have poetry

Who felt the itch of becoming
plucked each new feather

And stuck around,
filled the emptiness
with other beasts.

Anger, like my mother,
Who did not have poetry
No words to tell me why.

2.

Mother, my wings are heavy
with beasts I have carried

As I have seen you do,
I learn by sight and feel,
and like you I am deaf to caution.

Mother, I have discovered a word
for those who fly away—*Wisdom*
Hope—for those who stay

3.

My daughter will be born a wingless thing
like her mother, like mine

I wonder if hers will sprout at all,
if she will fly—

Or, if woman after woman, the body
has forgotten how

Groundling,
Do not discard your wings,
hope alone will not provide

But should they never come
do not stick around
and place your anger
between blade and bone

Do not shoulder the empty beast
and stay.

My Groundling, remember
the house of your own embrace

Remember
your two feet
and walk.

SNAKE POEM / CENTO *after "Snake Poems" by F. X. Alarcón*

Come sister, Nightfall draws—

First, cross yourself
Watch: Even the dead are dancing

The whole scene: wound, blood, ribs
copal—*the blessed kiss*

When Jesus can't hear me,
A Yellow Woman, I look to
La Virgen / tells me to be more serpentine:
Renewal shall protect you

Each precious dawn: a landscape of flowers

Each morning another
Future: walk bare faced, naked

May rattlesnakes guide you

May you step lightly
In return
          do not forget this

Each ceremonial mile
Display the body compacted How *undoing*
the length of your esophagus unfolds a
path

to your mouth: now, a dry river bed
a delta, bared teeth—

Where you waited, so polite—   How *too long for*
Water, while

The season for rain   While Sister, asleep
Now behind us—

The year turns   we swallow dreams   heavy sink
Uncoiled spines into sand—
Prostrate
—How the desert snake prays, a nocturne
blind cipher for boulders

Come precious dawn,
Sister, dance—

The flowers
A landscape of rattlesnakes

All snakes
A field of flowers

All fields
A prayer for water

Water
A plea for the parched

Sister, dance!
:Rumba! Bomba! *Bolero!*

Como Volar—

Every ceremonial mile
Kickdirt, rise

Open, Dear Sky

Rain
The parched, forgiven

Ghosts
Your frantic dervish

Fish-scale
Bone-hungry
Dried-white

Sister,
Your remnants
Trail-Shed

Serpentine,
Your wake—

HALF LIFE
One cannot get around the assumption of reality, if only one is honest.
—Albert Einstein

My father walks—out somewhere in this world he weaves in and out of my dreams halting reels from a silent movie. I am a proof, a projector. I am his negative, his ghost. contact transfer. silver halide. a mirror, backward. splitting image. revolving door, like celluloid. like grain. like light, but mold. like long division. but rot. leak, but decay. heat. fade. bleach. fire. like forest burnt warm—

But soft, softer still. twilight. until haze. until downy fuzz, until windowsill. until dust, until sunbeam. because entropy. because eyes.

Because thermodynamics. because music. because weed. because wool. because waves, also particles. because scarce. because Schrodinger. because *The Lion King*.

Because I don't know how to love them better.
Their cigarettes and pea coats.
I have been halved and halved and had.

But I got this far, Dad; on half an origin story
Half made-up biology. Half, playing house—

daddy soft palate
daddy underbelly pierced, pitched
daddy leaden, I carry you beneath my tongue
have not yet made up my mind

Anything is probable, until you flip the house lights
define it otherwise. Ask the cat.

He decays at an exponential rate.
My father: halved and halved and halved
He knows—

Please don't ruin the surprise. No peeking.
Somewhere unobservable; Here, and long gone,

My father is alive.
My father is dead. My father
is alive. My father is dead.

RED NAME

Mother named me *Soon*—
Obedient daughter, filial

Faithful dog, soft
Pink

My Father's
Humid
Lap

Did not speak
Did not mouth
Dead thing

Alone
Unhinged
Jaw

Gnawed each piece
Crowned Myself

Sunrise
Buried
Prayed

Night
Torn open,

Worn,
Unholy Spine

Fashioned
Gloves

Tongued
Meat from
Nail

Swallowed
Buried
Prayed

Exhumed
My Red
Name

Bone
Adorned

Rubied
String

Aubergine
Globule

My Red Name
Enrages
My Mother

My Red Name
Refuses
My Father

Soon
My Red Name
Burns—

Avert
My Red Name
Sees—

Hunts
Jaw
Dangling

Devoured
Many men

Prayed pink

Earned
My Red Name

Finally—

Dinner, Daughter
Father, Viscous
Mother, Master

Soon, *Sun*
Sunrise, Soon
Soon, Gone

A PIGEON IS A ROCK DOVE

Before poetry
Grandmother taught me to pray
Hallowed be thy name—& lost her mind.

>*Her solemn back curled form;*
>*I, child, one eye cracked*

My Grandmother lives in the shelter of my undoing
Holds my hand, asleep; contained

Within her dreams my heart—
break: her black eyes grey

Her hair white all
at once.

My Grandmother all dreamspeak. Up
She floats, reels the popcorn ceiling & back
breaks heavy, glass mind shatters my bedroom

My Grandmother, shelter while
I unraveled

My Grandmother, sheltered
Unravels—

>*All Pigeons are Rock Doves*

Someone told me, symbolic
of peace and good news

Blessed are the meek
Sky rats flock a pizza crust.

I feel for the one: footless straggler
Torn wing, nubbed flutter

Worse for wear
by way of broom
by tire or swift kick

—I cheer for that one:

>*Ain't dead yet,*
>*Good for you, Bud.*
>*Don't need feet to fly, Bird—*

Mourning doves, they never
bothered me; dumb things,
all murmur & free.

They rush the tops of buildings all
at once.

What same circuitous thought
propels them?

What keeps my Grandmother
tethered

>*Hard bed & ceiling*

> *No TV, headache*
> *No sleep, all horses, legs fused*
> *& bow tied.*

Determined beatific thing won't you let go?
Oh, pathetic, gentle

> *Hobbler, I cheer for you*

At home we mourn too early.

In dreams she walks through walls,
Tells me:

> *No sleep, headache—*
> *Shouts and incantations, all horses*
> *Old histories, these legs bowed to God*

In the morning, My Grandmother sees birds on the
Ceiling

Describes them the same. Asks:

"Aren't you tired, Pigeon?
Don't you want
to stop?

Let go
& rest now

Gentle
Dove?"

[II]

If I were a superhero I would talk to cities. Maybe to hear it say five more minutes, come back to bed. Some feral hound nuzzling its way between us. I think of all the parts of me I am losing. How none of it makes me stronger, just different. I wonder if I'll ever be myself again. And if not, why would that be such a bad thing.

—**Jason Bayani, "Locus"**

SAVE ME SAN FRANCISCO

Today is Monday and
I was born two days ago.

I want to apologize but
What for?

This strange betrayal
This lightness of being: my wet towel heart wrung
over a city

I thought would save me.   *April showers!*

in San Francisco
The weight of you lingers.

My dry heart hung
I ghost up & down sidewalks

feather light sternum: empty birdcage
the bottoms of my feet, indoor palms pale white
and skyward—

I am a prayer, perhaps.

Hovering supine, the magician's assistant, Sputnik
weaving streets and alleys—hills and secret stairwells
North and South of Market St.

I'm told this place can make a cat of a girl, rewind time
a little bit; that strange things still exist, secrets tucked

Between tourists & tech workers
Pocket magnetized, abuzzing sunshine

& sidewalk pawing grace
Softer landings, please—

I was told this place would change a girl—

NOTES FROM HUBBLE'S DREAM I:

I've heard, where you are, planetariums (whole cities)
stay open for dreamers.

The narcoleptic wander through multiversions,
other outcomes:

>   *Rabbits in a rowboat in the river moonlight.*
>   *A bridge of magpies, two lovers on their backs.*

Their half sleep *hello's*, a trade secret.
Open sesame, slippers and silk formalities.

& reverent, *hush* into a grand concourse
full of promise, *ad infinitum*—
This is how the lucid dream.

Where you are, taxi cabs make oceanic trips.
Trains slipstream through bedrock
from borough to borough. I've heard
that after rush hour   they fly.

Where you are, petals rain on Broadway, unannounced.
I've seen them—a frustration of sparrows,
that startled cow—waiting for the bus *goodbye* on Bowery

I know I told you I'd never be
owned, a manicured moon,
or your woman—

I was feeling cinematic at the time.
It felt like the right thing to say.
I'm sorry.

IDEATION

I am sick and tired
the outside kind
not just the body,
inside. Not just the bodies
inside my already dead
weight sopping wet body
the invisible mess sad sack
body who won't leave bed or
put on socks probably
what let inside the outside
sick in the first place now
the inside sick comes on
slowly sometimes all at once
it's been a steady baseline
sorrow a foundational ache
most my life lately
I've been thinking in ways
I haven't in a long while
I'm driving across the
bridge for instance toward
San Francisco and I imagine
myself making a hard left
over and over I see the hurtle
toward the division concrete
I see the sky and then I consider
a more practical dismount for
a while I thought about jumping
then pills I thought about hanging

here but things are different now outside
I've started taking the bus to work inside
they've become something else entirely—

STARS WITH TEETH

Treacherous stars pluck each
diamond replace them with teeth;
because nobody wishes on teeth.

They fall like stars do, sure, but teeth grow back
unlike stars; and we don't want people sold on easy
commodity / wishes you can trade for a dollar.

CALIFORNIA

I'm here,
in bed before the sun goes down.

The West Coast is wasted on me. It's February
the girl next door is wearing shorts.

Last night was an orange.
I mean, the moon is an orphan.

I promise I will not
board another Greyhound outbound
point my toe at other cars
& call them my new friends.

I've rearranged myself, since.
I don't think it's a phase.
I am not scared or certain. Sure,
I was yours. But I let you let me go.

Here, the night is an orange.
I mean, the moon is an orphan,
and so temporary are we.

The moon creeps away from Earth.
Our oceans will die one day.

You have always been
so beautiful.

And, I let you let me go.

But, maybe
maybe you'll remember:

You let me get away—

WHAT HAPPENS WHEN DEPRESSION IS NO LONGER YOUR SINGULAR UNIVERSE. (*the truth about black holes*)

We don't talk much about Hell, repurposed:

>(What happens when depression is no longer
>your singular universe)

Once a God particle, less ornate, now.
Charcoal dull, still dense, a singularity

>they made you swallow

Not to discount or overuse the term
Certainly there are worse things—

you must remind yourself

 —than your eating habits.

Some days you can't remember
what they are.

>You could point to the wormhole,
>right here

But what would that prove?

>It's been there, *Reptile Brain*
>since the dawn of your trajectory.

Hell is a body part, now.

Skin and bone exoplanet.
Neutron star, sternum scar.
It catches your seatbelt, you
off guard, every time.

Mind the gap:

Make eye contact, smile.
Notice symptoms, durations.

Nod if you understand.

Heave yourself
           No, ease your way
off another moving vehicle. Cross
six humming lanes. *Wait for it:*

              [a brisk walk
              and a light jog
              are not the same thing]

Remember how you lost your head
at the front door, how Tetris felt like Pac-Man.

You will cry in public. You will want to
drive yourself off a bridge from time to time.

Arrive early:

You will trip the alarm
for the rest of your life.

Mind the time
it will take
to explain
this scene.

                    TSA: *So much traffic—*

The god particle you swallowed a neutron star
broke the scanner.

                    Butterflied your sternum.

Can't stop tonguing the wound—
that large black hole:
                in x-ray
                            after x-ray,
                                            after x-ray

[III]

We are concerned that you are learning self-empowerment
without self preservation

—**Ariel Gore, "We Were Witches"**

LAST SEASON ON

Gently, now. I am not-strong, unarmed, no Bigfoot plot twist. I've come undone, it seems. Fresh out of platitudes, nothing up my sleeve, I didn't mean to show up empty-handed, or this frantic. *I'm sorry.* You see, I was spotlit
when the pilot crashed. They called me out. They canceled me. I lost my mind but I trust you now. Would you pin in a lineup? Have you come here to feed?
   Here comes the inevitable transmogrification: are you here to lead the mob to me? Have you seen a girl split
this easy? Would you like to see a parlor trick? *I'm sorry.* I needed you bloodied, hunting
red herrings. I needed you twisted, believing in monsters. You didn't see this goldfish coming:
it was me. So charmed by indiscretion I'd convinced us lovers. I missed my mark. I missed your monologue *how real we were*, how primed for—the violin rise, the ice cold staccato, the happy ending cut for time. The body count, the dolly back, the brutal denouement: ribs blown open, hearts aborted. Last scene screaming *we were made for each other!* Laid bare, limbs splayed, *everybody* watching. You and I
were quite the pair, so brief and monstrous—   *so gross and so very special.*

PET SOUNDS [*Dear Valentine*]

You call me your: Oxytocin, Serotonin, Dopamine Dream
Girl Norepinephrine Nightmare, Drama Queen

Rapid Cycling Mood Shifter, Horse Powered Trigger Finger
Your hopelessly addicted, eroded smirk

I broke your brain, Love—
You broke my heart.

TO DO LIST
Unpacking my failings upon realizing that the dog is old and will die one day—

1.

You've weathered worse.
Perhaps you've forgotten
Living can be more than survival—

Your grandmother in her empty room
talking to ghosts and
smoke alarms

    Call your mother.

The dead rat collapsed, edging
gardens you'd meant to plant,
tomatoes on a dying vine

—more than the accumulation of
regrets at summer's end.

Why entertain ghosts, unbegun? She's here
sniffing the breeze—*fall is coming.* She turns
thrice, elated, moving with the sun.

Content to be—

Which is more than you've been allowed
these long days, alone. Someone to say:

    It's alright; wherever you're headed, keep going

And who else but the dog loved you
without a list of conditions?

> *Of course you met them, worked hard*

They say it happens quick. The death
of what you love is never timely, always
inconvenient.

It isn't her fault you lost a job.

> *No, not her fault. He waited*
> *Five years to unmask a monster.*

2.

Monday your mother
offers to bargain on your behalf. The world
is unfriendly, what good are we, alone?

> *But mom, love is not a temple*
> *built of knees.*

So you haven't made the short drive home
scared of other silences
she's tucked into the lines
gathered around her mouth:

> *You are too old to be wanted.*

And yours:

Are no more than a failed decade,
a few poems.
Call your mother

Slips further down
your life as told in to-do list.

3.

So you named a man *Home*.
Forgot that home is a construct,

and stayed while he took mallet to foundation
renamed you: rubble heap, broken tile girl

Did you let her age before she was due?

3 odd decades, the misplaced trust, the punctured
disappearances, your empty hands once too busy
playing house in other bodies.

And just in time to face the letdown, time to watch them fade
To mourn the slow wither of their respite:

Your mother's hands, like yours.
How your grandmother sang your name.

4.

Everyday:
- Breakfast
- Wipe both eyes clean

- Change soiled clothing, sheets
- Spoon feed, play airplane
- Restore what vision you can

Yours of them, theirs of you.

Could you stick around this time,
wave them each out of sight?
Stay should they return?

You've weathered much.
Perhaps you have forgotten—

Bend the way your Mother taught you.
Talk to God like Grandma does.
Move with the sun, turn thrice.

—their forgiveness, the quick
and loving pardon. Perhaps
you'll remember, now:

This is Home.
This is what it means to Love.
*This is what matters. Only thi*s.

EFFIGY

The corners of my bed smell like different men I've invited to help me forget you, to mask your scent.

Bottom left, the artist whose name I forget. His large, rough hands that smelled like turpentine and clay.

That baby-faced bartender who left bite marks on my thighs, then kissed them back to bruise.

The bank teller, his blue shirt and ugly tie wrapped around my neck twice, pulled tight then flung; he fucked—body hard, deathmatch loud—a brawler, like you.

The bed undone, nasty, snarling—I could dismantle the frame—bare hands and teeth; I could wring out the sweat and bodies but won't. Let the odors seep through, let the stench permeate—anything to drive you out.

Last week, I fucked a guy because you share a name. I wanted to scream it over and over at the ceiling, rake it up and down his spine like I used to yours. It was almost the same. I let him in twice and scratched you a letter bright red into his back.

I wake up naked, always alone. This morning I noticed a jagged burn, a curious destruction. I tug it fast and tear a hole, look inside. It is space enough to bury my fist-sized heart. I consider it.

There was that college kid, linguistics, eager to do it; kept saying do it, only to stammer something thereafter about soccer and homework and Dustin

Hoffman—his face flushed, panting, his pants still around his ankles; O! His mismatched socks! I bought him a six-pack and drove him to his dorm room.

Yesterday, I kissed a father of two and left him in a Walgreens parking lot after we did it in the back of his Saab. Fucking elsewhere seemed beside the point and I just wanted to go home.

For months I craved you. I mourned you in celibacy, as though it would make a difference. I wallowed in your pillowcase, to smell you where I could; to burrow and coil myself around you, to say: belong to me—the way animals speak with their bodies.

Strawman, I made home, I nested; I waited and waited—

Look, I don't love you anymore. I just want to feel human again.

I almost did with a man who offered me breakfast; real slow.
I let him lean into the soft and raw.
We danced in the kitchen, and he was gone by morning. Hating him reminded
   me of you.

Strawman, I've fucked myself into a maze.
All the aching corridors lead to your center.

Last night, I dreamt of you: an opened palm, a fist shaped heart, my new Saab—
A world tucked inside our disjoint, curled, coiled to spring
Our breaths in sync, mammal hearts beating.

Strawman, light the pyre. Burn on high, O sternum!
Smoke rise, burnt hair, throw the heart's wild pack off course—
Your head in my lap, dirty sheets, the acrid stench of want and mistake.

Can't wash you off, unzip this skin, fistfuls where you linger—I've tried.
Every gasping breath, choke, a gasoline reminder:

Your scent is in everyone, in goddamned everything—

PATRON SAINT OF THE LOST CAUSE

No sinners in this town; not a single saint I've seen
Terrible Angels, Demonized Androids, Abandoned Homes—*sure*

I like the Questionable Weirdos. Sometime-believers. Past-life card sharks
Penny tails up, facedown in the dirt.   I know what I'm looking for.

Pick-up games, nameless strays: long-stretched always hungry
for attention—   They collect at 7-Elevens

At the church of friction,
At the hairline fracture—
                              at *Hallelujah*

Where ancient meridians touch
Where pleasures sing bright through my body

Back by the old Motel back by the
freeway off-ramp

No Saints. Just self-destructive city kids, neon fuckups.
The collared, after curfew.

Their cigarette tips, sodium vapor lit
Eyeballs shining, quick to forgive, forget
They quiver in earnest.

Going on and on
About on and on and *on*

So forth *on*
All night   *and on*

In earnest—

FIREWORK

Some of us are forged in flame, borne of ash
& dynamite (I have heard) explosive
& one afternoon, meandering
perhaps at a bus stop, waiting
alone at a traffic light, maybe
we will alight, pulse
flicker then boom—

While others glance polite
straight ahead, thinking:

How lovely
such fire—
works

(The rain of ash)

How lovely
the fire—
flies

THIS IS A POEM ABOUT CLIMATE CHANGE

Our last fight
both of us fucked
on acid, & the bathroom fan?
—madness.

Someone outside screaming: *do you even know
where we are right now?*

De-escalation is a handy trait
but how could you say: I love you—
& mean it?

The moment is past, anyway
you see it now don't you, Love?
We're history.

We did this to ourselves we
saw it coming, the old wives' tale
repeated adage, our mothers unresolved
& jumped, regardless—

The plumage
    The flume
        This furnace
            These feathers
                How cliché.
Please don't leave that part out.
We were doomed from the start.

Disrupted weather patterns
this whole clusterfuck—

Hey, Future Dweller, Nostalgic Robot,
this body this world this
whole thing is a trap.

Nothing thrives here.

Don't bother.

TERMINOLOGY

1.

Can't stand small talk. *Listen*:
the heart is no object
of rational pursuit. It was never

Love: just another stand against
restraint, another testament to need,
to compulsion, to lazy writing— *Anyway*,

I fancied myself an exit sign, skirt-hiked
stilettoed heeler, the town mirror, lightning struck.
I was powder-soft, a maniac spared the rod.

It's no secret: *I was fabulous*—
It's no secret: You fooled me.
No secret how easy

I fold and fold again. I've lost
sight of the seams. Undone, I fell
asleep, lost my teeth, stopped counting.

What good am I, half alive?
a pretty mouth, expiring?

2.

I knew you were a red flag
eyeliner streaks on motel sheets,
the crisp starch of anonymous mornings.

I thought you were a Thursday night
learned too late on Sunday.

Once, your face was everything
I needed to be found.

You are still a thousand names: *Right here,
now and never again.*

You used to make me laugh
the way only I can—

MOST BIRDS DO NOT MATE FOR LIFE. NOT EVEN A GENUINE PAIR BOND.

Keloid:

>Your fissure is your rose is your river mocks you
>Try to be smaller
>Unseen, sink
>
>Your heart slips, you sleeve
>Your scar map, the stars
>Fault line & drill
>
>Rings on a tree,
>Dead ringer,
>*Ranger*—

Fault:

    Past lives gone
    a wry heart worn broken

    Finch on my forearm
    another bird stoned dead

    Red-handed
    Pair-bond unbound
    dead half flown
    & my half in-hand

    Our once shared dangers, *Roger—*
    Dodger

    Consider yourself armed
    Consider yourself just moments
    Consider yourself contrarian

    Careful enemies, all

    Blackbirds do not mate for life

    Curves and trip—
    wire, *Romeo*

Fissure:

    Crows—They smell you,
    come

    All men, dogs; the bloody
    drip—dry

    All faults stoned calcified still—
    water, eternally metallic

    Copper, sink.
    Smell

    The Red-handed, come.
    Spill.

    The Iron-fisted, come.
    Cursed.

    Bone clipped, teeth
    clatter, nerves ticking thumbs
    all tongues clacking

    The pot boils, meat
    Pilfered.

    Haunted, hunted
    You, haunched

    Bone-cursed, coursing

    Blood *Cursing*

IRON MAIDEN

Mouth of mercury
Shadow of teeth

Metal and bone
Terminator hungry

Devotee,
You are here to eat

Ribs blooming black
Flower where you broke
Skin

Fault you left the heart
Found the lungs—*delicate*

Pomegranate blossom
Skyward; split white mouthful
        —Jewel stain

Inhale the tender
Mouth the bloodied mouth.

Kiss this Iron Maiden

Her turn to devour—

BLOOM

Take your time. Don't
Wake the dawn. Look

Not a petal
disturbed: a just-peaked bloom

                       & snip:

Your Centerpiece

Her pretty head, severed
One deft pinch
It hurts to be beautiful

                 Like a broken nose
                 Like being stripped

Worse to be ignored

                       ☼

Carefully prune the node

Delta where esophagus meets
& two fingers kiss

Sternum collars, shoulders gather
indent—soft, *soft*
                 —*right* there

☀

Pray, resplendent flower,
Incant a ritual for rain; hum air into
Notes she cannot hit

        She clips

☀

The Swan Necked Stem
Squat vase ready, dying

        Chin up, Blossom!

Chirp the Devotees
They peel open her lips, slip trinkets
Past her teeth—for good luck, a brilliant cease

        A choke
        A smile
        An apology
        An eruption
        Applause

Such perfection—

☀

Once, I
Face toward the sun
Swallowed a stone.

The nicked, zippered
Esophagus sliced red
Cascade unfurling

Plucked a bird from thin air
Denied it flight, its feathers
fistful by fist

Wore its plumage
Promised it a different brilliance:
                Survival, Sacrifice,
                Cunning, Shine

Lies & fancy talk:
                Unarmed her
                Skinned her
                Forced her
                Fight

Funny, isn't it?

Potpourri Princess
Beheaded Aviary
Veiled Hysteria

Like the time you called to me:

                "Love" &

Stripped me bare.
Left me on display.

END OF LEASE

A whole year gone by—
On the anniversary of the death of us, I crushed myself   like a pill bug:
laughable armor but brave, still

And slept forever, or wished I did, the dog curled,   my small concavity.

The sun is out now; they say
Spring is here. And I was born two days ago   For the first time

      felt reason to unfurl. Imagine that: my body a
celebration.

Hasty: an acceptance

The days grow long. And I was born two days ago;   practically afloat.
Winter shed. Watershed. Ache and bone extracted   *of you*

Today is Monday. And I was born two days ago.   I feel I should
apologize but

What for?

[IV]

Wubba Lubba Dub Dub
—**Rick Sanchez,** *Rick & Morty* **(S1:EP5)**

LUCID DREAM

Davy Jones's Lover. Sidewalk after a storm.
So many names for a broken vessel: a hull, a shell, a hairline
fracture, a seam come loose. A bruise—

Six-car pileup. So many names for a wreck. The door in your chest
Sometimes a gap Others a canyon Never an exit
Strategy: no say over open or close,   just lonely.
Write what you know. Just lonely. Write that
You aren't just lonely. Are a crease. An easy fold.
High functioning. Overwhelmed. Bolt cutter.
First overboard should the boat sink. Jumper.

You wake up drowning, every morning.
The ocean in your chest bemoans you:

> *If the earth would hold still a moment*
> *Still the churning. Reclaim a center.*
> *Control my momentum. Stave the anxiety*
> *Enjoy a whole day—such momentous occasion!*
>
> *Imagine if it would—*

ALBATROSS

I remember nothing.
Dead girl afloat in the thick
and vicious, so viscous.

I see you, Ancient Mariner.
Go ahead old man; it's me.

This is my skin, gut clean.
my bones, my mid and cross sections.

The human body is a marvel, can hold much
and more. Example, I

rearranged by kinder hands am still
recognizable by incision, by the man
who made me. Example, I

once a basement corner, a water heater
pilot through the dark. It was my fault
the boat capsized, the crew died.

Spin, all scars now. Another story:
Once, I made a stunning bride
eyes wide, wild for you. They want to know

Your version: an unlucky flourish
reduced me. A dead bird,

mouth sewn shut, sitting pretty. Never
the center of a storm. You liked best
my game face, my stubborn lack of transparency.

They want to know why
you've returned. Why
I remember nothing. Why

Dead Girls remember nothing.

PSYCHOPOMP

Name your rivers, mark each one different
Dig nails into their banks, become a bridge elsewhere

Your laughter is an abandoned vessel
You consider this turn of phrase, look away

& I, after nights without sleep stumble over your vertebrae
Forget to be gentle, lost in all that supposition:

Someone else's mouth disavowing
My own

Counting new knots in my back
Your interest in syntax—*what new sounds!*

More nightmare rhetoric—*apocalypse, paralysis*
Every shitstorm & snore thereafter,

the same synaptic mantra:

This is the apocalypse & I am paralyzed
This is the apocalypse & I am paralyzed

OCTOBER

Last October there were seven hours of light and you spent them asleep or in love with a man with two hearts: one tucked deep in the crook of his arm
the other in the doorway of his house

Hangman, he offered but you dodged the needle and thread snuck past the blood rope and tender organ. You sat on his chest, peered down his throat for a wormhole, pounded sternum for his real age—

Cold ache of a wooden floor, you made love to revive him
Saw his heart pulse
                —just out of reach

Exhausted, took shelter in the curvature of his spine
while he slept and swore through the winter

Sat vigil. Suffered. The heart in the door still
stubborn throbbing

Cursing the flies—the swarms that gathered
around it

would not yet come inside.

I REFUSE

I am tired
of loving hard
& letting go.

I do not want
to love anything
difficult, anymore.

I am aware
I am a difficult
Creature—*thing*.

I am aware
of pots & kettles.

I have learned to love
under condition & hard hat.

I have been to the basement
and back.

Gave my all to a revolving door
My heart up for demolition.

Sat waiting for a beam to snap,
An exit sign, a condemnation

For fear of breaking a man—*What faith!*
These small, pointless hands?

SALAD DAYS *3/31/21*

1.

What do you say to Memory
when it shows up welcome
for a change?

How do I say: *Hello friend,
how long will you stay?*

When I say *Love*, do I mean
whatever love means, now?

When I run into the past: *where are you going?
Can I come too?*

One mustn't trust it, Memory
is soluble, is a wrinkle, a rewrite,

a liar at your door. Something about
retraced footsteps, grooves on a record
with no tracks to show;

But every recollection you can't put down,
every dog eared repetition comes back
grinning, having made itself example—

POP QUIZ:
        When I say Love do I mean
        whatever love means, now?

Correct Answer:
> *I can still feel your hands in mine.*

Incorrect:
> *I'll forget how warm, when I quit thinking*
> *about you all the time.*

2.

This poem is about Memory & Meaning
while I should be moving on.

About disregarded hours, swamp cooler drip,
the ancestry of familiar songs, years later.

About two AM bodega runs, cigarette
summers too hot to fuck.

About tall cans of Arizona Iced Tea
rolled across a sticky lover's neck,

the Chinatown bus
and the February doldrums.

This poem is about Snowmageddon, Sandy.
This is about hitchhiking the Williamsburg Bridge.

About the summer sun, bisecting 34th street
Manhattan dripping gold, cross-sectioned—

How it all goes on
without me.

3.

We walked all night that summer. Slept all day.
If we sat too long, you got too thoughtful;
or I got sad.

SoHo through Hell's Kitchen, sky high
heels on cobblestone; shrieks and peals of laughter

from dusk:
>   *When the sun slips past the Hudson*
>   *kisses the ass-end of Lady Liberty*

'til dawn:
>   *When it comes back around*
>   *measures two fingers above the Sugar Factory—*

Even east, Odd west I chased your number
past Washington Heights. I still read your letters from Alphabet City
about the Spa Castle in Flushing, the soccer fields at dawn
beneath the Queensborough Bridge.

I miss ourselves, back then,
out all night, just waking up.

The Limelight is a mall, now.
Max Fish is gone. My dog's breath smells like Canal street
after six. Everybody moved to Silver Lake

(*and kids, these days*)

But this poem is about disco fries for breakfast
and bodega coffee

How clever we were,
how kind—

5Pointz and the Norteño buskers, heading west on the 7.
The guy who sang *Over the Rainbow* at the Lorimer L.

Daylight over the Pulaski, the sun in your hair.

How do I tell you—

These ever-further thens and theres
make more sense to me, still.

You can't hear me
long gone west with the sun

Though I keep looking
back east to find you.

AT THE MOTEL BEHIND THE DENNY'S

I mean / I understand
mourning's rules:

Love & minor chords   I'm sorry
sound either/or   I missed you.

Sing to me, please /

    About the moon-a and the june-a and
    the spring-a—

pickup   stations:

    The way you smile just beams
    The way you sing off key—

Please don't begrudge
my silly distractions.

                    TV blasting
motel closed the pool I know
your voice in distant traffic
in stray transmissions, our
mixed
signals: wayward coast to coast

You know,
I think I liked
our close proximity

What it was like
to share a grid,
a shower—

How quiet
this world feels lost
how I feel the same

quiet, but different.

YOU MIGHT BE DEAD OR DREAMING

1.

Obsessed with the technicalities
of memory, the limits of rhetoric,
she refuses to chew or swallow

The traveling lump, negligible details
no food, no breath

until she performs.

2.

A woman's body
moving dark. The third rail sparks.

Shapes not skin, shadows not color
The body stops here.

Dead girl on a moving train. Make
the patrons look away.

3.

The trick is not
to force the fingers, to pry
past the teeth.

4.

The dogs we dumped in the ravine
Returned last winter. Whole droves,
not undead, but their skins clinging
and limp

Her German Shepherd, paws
gone and a broken neck

—tail wagging.

5.

Press either
side of the jaw, hold the mandible.
when the lips part, keep the tongue
from blocking the tube.

6.

Those who perished in the subway fire
lit and translucent. Brighter than the
street light, brighter than the head lamps,
wandering home.

7.

If there is spit, wipe.
If there is blood, hold.

8.

Trick is not to breathe
trick is to grit down and bear it
fake the wriggle and the limp
until you are alone.

9.

If food is consumed, reward.

10.

The emotional capacity to change course
inherent in all—

What's the difference?
We could have gone home all along.

We didn't.

NOTES FROM HUBBLE'S DREAM II:

I love you with the violence of brand new: gas and spark, hot swarm
babbling incoherent, exponentially—

Too hard and fast and much: I have loved you *nebulously*
petulant with want: a *big . fat . baby.*

My love makes spectacle of *whole* galaxies crashing
Makes *disaster* a gentle nudge on a planet's axis.

I love you on a tightrope, precariously—

Everything about us is all and nothing,
a fucking disaster, a game of hearts &
fracture.

Lovers like us: flammable, inflammable
Lovers like us: sweet kindling, blazing

Kaboom and particle, whole cities
leveled by lovers like us

Destroyers of worlds

[You + I]

I went on a date with a man
Who doesn't like space documentaries.

I miss the old you, always
exploding

No matter who saw: arms crossed,
atoms colliding

A whole scene: shooting stars, ending
planets over nothing

[Absolutely nothing.]

QUANTUM ENTANGLEMENT

This world has destroyed itself
Readjusted
Countless times

Here we are
Regardless

Intertwined,
Particulate.

Quantum Maniacal

I have much to face
That I haven't
Don't want to
Make plans or
Promises—

                                      [What I know]
                                      I wait, gathered taut, ready
                                      While you sleep

                                      Open a window
                                      Your door will
                                      Slam

                                      When I become light
                                      So will you

I will burst
Into tears
Unexpectedly

[What I don't]
Whether you are my ghost
I/yours

Whether the heart / breaks
On the in-breath
Or the out—

ECHO CHAMBER

This hallowed worm. This hole in your chest. You've dubbed yourself *chasm*, Love. And I, the apple of your needle and thread, an eye, an arrow home: the sticky sweetness of a wet mouth pierced, rotting fruit still a meal; and I, a heart, worn—broken, *Sugar*. Inside you are holy and inside you are poison and soft inside you are a cavity. And I, an invasive species, *Sweetheart*. Inside you I am home. Inside you, I have found an alchemy: turned poison into prison into isotope to a solitude blooming wide taking room inside you I am as vast as the sea, pungent as the fruit too heavy to hold, a bone-white drying, a dead tree still leans into the cold high twist and gnarls its whole form a fist of branches or hands outstretched to praise its state, stalled or evolving, regardless—inside you I was twisted, once. I was afraid, once, feigned dancing. Once I could not give or take more space, I wised up, shrunk to size and small and learned that lonely does not mean alone or incomplete, even without. So, I bore down further inside the seam undid the void between lift and lid and lie and found whole worlds stacked within within within my particularities—*elementary*—discovered multiplicities, capitals, necropoleis, canyons, tomes of unresolved cosmologies and puzzled parts I'd pulled apart—each lonely facsimile, smiling, still. I caved. I cried. I melted glaciers a long time. Now, I am a softer landing, I am a solemn magic, necessary, no longer borne of need. I have always been worthy. I mean to say: inside the doors inside your head lies another hole another vaulted heart asleep it dreams of float and of flight of deep-down an untouched you holier than you and I then, and now, older than eternal, ephemeral, and deeper still, you and I an echo chamber, a hall of mirrors: you and I staring wide at one another and another and another and—

[V]

Ten long trips around the sun since I last saw that smile, but only joy and thankfulness that on a tiny world in the vastness, for a couple of moments in the immensity of time, we were one

—**Ann Druyan**

MY GRANDMOTHER DREAMS

In her dreams I am a child I am her granddaughter her final masterpiece. In her mind I go to church with the suitors she has dreamt for me—their slick, combed hair and black suits—in her mind we are not beholden to time, her love is alive and she hasn't gone mad for another forty years—

In her dreams my Grandmother is a small girl, annexed; a woman, a half-finished country. She is beside herself at the playground with her granddaughters, watching them play, such joy and contentment. Her eyes are dark and sharp, not milky grey, and she remembers each detail; weaves the world a story as she has taught me to do—

She remembers how long her braids how bent her spine how picked over the bodies alongside the road: the whine of an air raid, her eyes closed tight, just her hands and God to guide her. how the heart can be halved by a fence, a demarcation. how a mother knows the outline of her dead son, so still. how each passing decade, the world burns indiscriminate, hotter; and her body shrinks, less a shield. How her past is rootless, ruthless. how she worries for her children, and their children and—

In her dreams there is time and place and reason; there, my Grandmother is a child again, an ancestor, an amalgamation of all lives lived—woman after woman—each wondering when She stopped having the answers, stopped believing that things would work out in the end.

OSIP MANDELSTAM'S EGG —*after Malena Morling*

"*Is there a hall that contains the sky . . . but at dusk smeared with its own blood? . . . Do you think you will find your own mind in there, free at last from its 84,000 delusions?*"

Ever fit your foot or fist inside an egg?
Never mind the spatial limitations.

Hall full of possible
What did you have in mind?

Blind-eye the cracks in plaster. See the dead
vines creeping in?
I hate it when people say: *you have to crack
a few eggs to make an omelet. Or: she's a few eggs
short of a dozen*—

Once upon a time, a different almost
Somebody left

this brittle Fabergé. Unformed,
a bright idea perhaps

Dribbles yellow from the hairline.
Unformed, broken is the expectation

Nothing lasts. Last meals spoil
You turned out brittle.

And the mind is brutal
Believe me

You'd find it better served poached
and timid; undressed, spoon-fed

Imagine a hall that contains the sky
Imagine a daily air raid

& at dusk an armistice. The nightly cease
Imagine if you will

The good sleep. This brief assembly
The Dead, The Dead, The Dead eventually

AUBERGINE

We are
working animals—keep moving.

She first noticed on the 7 train, a
crimson sliver imperceptible but for the warm

Smear just inside her right knee, stained her
fingers pink when she licked her thumb and wiped
away the first—

She glowed a whole season, soft pink. Her face, her hands
carried through the holidays, lit up like a Christmas
miracle. Put a bow on top when she told her lover.

Now February,
not big enough to command a seat
in a sardine can, the metal pole

Steady the door lurching
onward bodies like
swine to slaughter—

Alone: pink, tender wet, milk white
recovery room wall pink-thin blanket.

The kid to her right with his tonsillectomy *the same node*

Sent home with diapers   *the furious irony*
and told to come back   *if it doesn't pass*

O! Little Anvil.
Irreparable Wound.

Same weight and size
palm small. Pink
like scar

She found Home on his knees
hiked her dress up:

> *Sorrow, ankle deep*
> *person in pieces you cannot see try*
> *and find the face, the teeth, you won't.*
>
> *Watch!   Do not avert your eyes.*
> *Do not avert your anything.*

Choked the wet from her throat.
Wailed like a woman excavated.

Sent him away—Home, a ruin
folded neatly, tissue white. A woman halved

Blooming nothing pink
or brilliant, just unbegun

Patted the earth with two hands, crossed
it out of books and mind

Promised it a name—

AMISS

I am first thing in the morning.
I am halved by bedtime.
I am five pills a day.

I am your breath, caught.
I am choke and sputter.
I am the lump in your throat.

I am summer's last tomatoes,
jewels on a dying vine.
I am a final offering.
I am no next time.

I am the swath of birds aloft.
I am the congregation startled.
I am the cow on your sidewalk
at breakfast.
I am the milk carton, appalled.

I am a serial monogamist.
I am the lure of house and home.
I've thrown out the urge to settle down.

Months since we've moved apart—
Missing since the holidays—
I am still amiss.

I am the nape of your neck,
someone else's morning altar.

I am too small to mind the gap.
I am harmful if swallowed.
I am a fracture left untreated.

I am bruise.
I am ghost.
I am disappearing.

I am cigarettes, your bad habit
leftover.

I am the drag and pull.
I am the ragged breath.

PRAYER FOR THE SEASON

I am a woman, abated, a city block upturned.
Four-alarm fire, tongue held in a cage match,
I am a phone call refused, an exceptional façade

    It takes a village to raise a monster

I am a whole village razed.

    Oh, Executioner,
    Show me how she got inside
    Show me where the fire started
    Show me where I lost my wallet

Where rot began, where fester
Left a bloodbath:

Whole auditoriums spellbound
Gasoline in the drain, heads severed all
Ventriloquists dragged & quartered
Tongue-evicted

Mumbled a tone-deaf Hosanna
Dumbfounded—*Lord, save us!*

    This world is open season

Whole intersections stopped
at massacre & crosshair. The
corners unaccounted—

Bless Our Valiant Failures, Late Bloomers
to the Schoolyard, The Sitting Duck, alone

    This world is open wound

Lord, Bless The Prodigal Arson
The Self-appointed Executioner,
The Vengeful, Sullen Queen
They come hunting—

Glory, their inheritance!
Pockets full of teeth & evidence

& Lord, Bless the rest of us
The Blissful Useless

    This world is open season

Easy Targets, split wide

    —open wound

& Won't you keep us
Helpless Onlookers?

Our best intentions
Our wrung hands,
Our rubbernecks?

DOG POEM

Most of us are terrible
with words. What we mean,
how we meant, what we needed
said instead

Dogs can be trained to speak, sing
at least a semblance. They say
the urge to please is marrow deep, *familiaris*

Most dogs get off on good behavior.
Though a prey drive: this instinct insatiable
Has been difficult to remove

I've seen the neighbor's mutt, brown bolt
ecstatic blocks and blocks shock collared
howling—*Squirrel!*—determined, still

Even the most amicable, most eloquent "Benji Franklin"
"Mister Noodles" or "Evelyn Woof"
will take off given the opportunity.

They can't help it. *Canis lupus*
This gives me hope.

Is there a trick to reassurance? An inflection, a hand gesture, to say—?
And of the times you are alone? When stillness is a pinprick, is a bed of nails,
is an ache without end or form—

When the words won't come and the worst keeps calling—

Look to the dog: old holdout,
guardian of your shared, wild past.
Proof that it was:

Her one eye opens, eyebrow raised—
Watches you stir or stay, unable to face
another morning.

It is true: the body fails us, as do words
but never the dog.

> Her weight against you, sturdy
> Promises to stick around, despite
> your failings—
>
> Her steady gaze, a wink
> a limp that recalls the old
> joy of a mad dash—

Nothing so beloved can be explained or lost, completely.

> Look: how good, how gentle
> how perfect she's made you.
>
> Unbeknownst to anyone,
> made loving an instinct.

It is true, the body fails us,
as we have failed so many others.

It is true, I am terrible with words
I regret much I cannot remedy.

It is true, we believe we can rid ourselves
of anything, the worst of it.

Little do we know: deep down, there are places
impenetrable to even us, good places
unyielding—

Though cunning as we have become
at folding the spirit to obedience.

[VI]

Katy

They say I mope too much
but really I'm loudly dancing.
I eat paper. It's good for my bones.
I play the piano pedal. I dance,
I am never quiet, I mean silent.
Some day I'll love Frank O'Hara.
I think I'll be alone for a little while.

—**Frank O'Hara**

ADMISSION

1.

I've hardly opened my mouth.

I don't share my name in case I'm made laughing stock;
I don't name things in case I lose my wallet.
I was turned off. I don't feel right. I am told otherwise.
I find confusion triggering. I admit I've tried to snap.

Tried to kick a girl into gear:
Rowed hard for the break and failed—shows over
How starved, how stretched, how thin
Skinned raw & dying to know better

I'll admit naming my guilty pleasures gets me off for one
Outsmarting yourself: *Congratulations!*
You've been double-blinded, foiled again—

I've planned a lunch date with my corrosions next weekend
It smells like pennies and lemon verbena in here

I'd pin myself in a lineup immediately—

Which one of you is to blame for all of it
this time?

2.

I've developed a taste for the difficult.

Born inauspicious
Mother dreamt the world a girl, knees skinned
A sheep's head crowning a wolf's mouth

Daughter raised for meat.

Sold heart-first to a confidence man Six
months in a bedroom Four in asylum last February
Etcetera　　　　　Honestly—

—*how* uncomfortable must one be to be
valuable and rare in this town? Paid any mind?

Attention! Another dramatic gesture ends in wild
encore.

Another public whimper—

3.

A piano from twelve stories up may be comedy,
given where it lands

Or tragedy, given the note

Have I misinterpreted myself again?
Have I missed my chance?

These once idle hands have been busy
keeping the doldrums at bay

Chopping it up for birds
between short circuits of flight—

Last night my Mother rearranged the world, again.
Awoke a meteor hurdling, a frantic wolf pack, she said
of bees: the whole dead swarm—

Packed & torched my suitcase. Warned
against skyscrapers, called them open doors
to the end

I've built a bunker for one.

Am I making any sense?

I didn't mean to interrupt
—to erupt like this at all

I still don't know what I'm doing

But I am trying

I am trying to understand
How I got here

How I ended up—

NAMESAKE

"Red sky at morning, sailor's warning. Red sky at night, sailor's delight." –Unknown

Note: my name in Korean is "No Eul". It is the common word for "Sunset". Specifically, it means "The Crimson Glow of Dawn and Dusk"

1.

Namesake, your hesitation lingers
pink horizon, a past already.

Sunset, daylight cannot be contained.
What is wild cannot be lost or claimed
by designation

An organized personhood is still of your own free will.
Getting out of bed *at all* is a display of hunger.

Walk long enough and far, you are bound to run
into your heart—*always*, the last place you look

      Here is your lover.
      Here is your home.

Here, your two small hands to hold
back an ocean, still the storm, to cry out

Namesake, your father is gone.
Endlessly moving West
—*move on*.

Do not shout for the echo back. Forget
The man who called you *unlucky*
called you a *failure where light forgot*—

Forgive the men
That you could not love
But foolishly tried. You are not wrong.

They were each bristled stiff.
Ready to wolf you whole
Heart and—

    Here is a dagger
    Do not spare another.

2.

Red Sky Come Morning,
the storms in your mind
are of your own making.

Look to your hands can quiet them.
Hands that kill and cure. Hands that pray
like children reach for other hands that span
the years between.

The slight of your hands, a testament to miracles.

Crimson Glow of Dawn and Dusk,
Here, you are a simple metaphor:

    Rush hour traffic.
    Another day's end.

            A nicotine trawl.
            The same sorry tread.

Elsewhere, you are the first slow blink
unfurling, color forerunning.
You are Blue.

rewarding the earliest of birds. Elsewhere
you have just begun to rose gold the sky.
Linger there, unnamed: *neither day or night*—

Where your father is a lover, careful
curtains drawn, a dawn, a promise
meant at the time.

Your mother is a dream
Her lonely spine peaceful
a silhouette unaware

You, her shadow
still asleep—

FRANK (*in conversation with "Katy" by Frank O'Hara*)

I've put my finger on it, *Katy*
you are dancing loud and clear.
I, too, am tired of grandstanding. My bones ache.
I want to draw large crowds in silence.
I ran out of things to say; and walked here, hopeful.
Someday I'll Love Christine No.
I think I've been alone for too long.

ACKNOWLEDGMENTS

"Bloom," "To Do List" —*The Rumpus*

"Visible Body," "At The Motel Behind The Denny's" —*Nomadic Journal*

"Reminder" —*Story Magazine*

"Elegy"—*Little Letters on the Skin* anthology

"Ideation" —*The City Is Already Speaking* anthology

"Lesser Gods" —*Harpoon Review*

"Origin Story" —*Vagabond Lit*

"Groundling," "A Pigeon is a Rock Dove" —*Entropy*

"Red Name" —*Bad Pony*

"Pet Sounds" —*Love Is the Drug & Other Dark Poems*

"This Is a Poem about Climate Change" —*ALTBEAST*

"Amiss" —*The Racket Journal*

"Snake Poem" —San Francisco Public Library "Poem of the Day"

"Snake Poem" contains lines from:
　Snake Poems: An Aztec Invocation (*Camino del Sol*) by Francisco X. Alarcón

"At the Motel Behind the Denny's" features lyrics from:
  "I Love to Singa" by Harold Arlen and E. Y. Harburg as performed by Johnnie Davis in the 1934 cartoon of the same title
  "They Can't Take That Away from Me" by George and Ira Gershwin

THANK YOU

Barrelhouse Books, *Quiet Lightning*, the *Rumpus*, Kearny Street Workshop, VONA, Red Light Lit, Nomadic Press, 16th & Mission, the American Film Institute, ARTogether.

Dan Brady, Matthew Carney, Dana Levin, Jason Bayani, Evan Karp, Paul Corman Roberts, Kim Shuck, Cassandra Dallett, Jennifer Lewis, Marisa Siegel, Noah Sanders, J. K. Fowler, Jason Ridler, Idan Levin, Blake Simpson, Artemisa Clark, Grey Rosado, Carmen E. Cottrell, Mom & Dad, Jesse Alejandro Cottrell, Ruthie Wagmore, Grandma and Brandeh.

ABOUT THE AUTHOR

Christine No is a Korean American poet, filmmaker, and daughter of immigrants. She is a Sundance Alum, VONA Fellow, two-time Pushcart Prize and Best of the Net Nominee. She has served as Assistant Features Editor for the *Rumpus*, as Fellow, then as a Program Coordinator for VONA. Currently, Christine is board member with Quiet Lightning, a Bay Area literary nonprofit and works as the Advocacy Program Manager at ARTogether, an organization committed to using art and storytelling to build and empower newcomer immigrant and refugee communities; and to promote healing, cultural humility, and intercommunity connection. She lives and works in Oakland, California with her dog, Ruthie Wagmore.